THRIVING DOG TRAINERS

AN INDISPENSABLE TOOL TO HELP YOU START OR REPAIR YOUR DOG TRAINING BUSINESS

TED EFTHYMIADIS

Thriving dog trainers

An indispensable tool to help you start

or repair your dog training business.

Published by Ted Efthymiadis
Halifax NS Canada
www.tedsbooks.com
Cover photo by Glenda Pearson

Copyright © 2018 by Ted Efthymiadis.
All rights reserved.

INTRODUCTION

This book is for two types of people:

- Aspiring dog trainers who want to avoid a lot of common pitfalls before entering the industry
- Current dog trainers who are struggling to make ends meet

This book is the product of many years of working in the dog training industry and many sleepless nights until I was taught *"The Formula."* Most dog trainers are not doing well financially and this book will unpack why. In 2017, the average full-time salary for a dog trainer was just $33,600 per year, and it doesn't have to be that way. It's unlikely that this book will blow your mind with technical jargon like unique sales propositions or minimum viable product, but if you like solid business advice written in easy to understand language, then this book is for you. *The Formula* is a method of starting or turning around a business that focuses on five principles which we will outline in this book.

1. Learn dog training skills
2. Pick the right business model
3. Find clients
4. Blow their minds
5. Get referrals

Big promises and shattered dreams

Mike's a dog trainer I met at a training seminar I was leading back in 2014. He's been training dogs full-time for about a year. He loves dogs; dogs are his thing. But things aren't going so great. He called me one beautiful summer day, and his voice was jittery; I could tell something was wrong. We didn't know each other well, but he needed my help and he knows I'm the kind of guy that loves to help. He's financially destitute. His wife was threatening to leave him and take the kids because she has to support him. A year ago, he promised her that if she would give him her blessing to leave his job, he would make enough money to support the entire family and she could leave the office job that she hated. Big promises and shattered dreams.

"Mike, I've got unlimited calling to the USA, I'll give you 4 hours of my time tomorrow night from 7-11pm." He agreed with a sigh of relief. Now, I didn't know Mike very well; really, I hardly knew the guy at all, but I've helped trainers from around the world turn their businesses around so I knew he could do it too. That night, I prepared a curriculum for him that would require a lot of changes. After our conversation that night, he completely changed his business, and in thirty days he went from making $1200/ month to $9000/ month. To this day, his business makes $6000-$10,000 consistently each month. The information I'm about to share with you changed his life forever and saved his marriage. If you take action on the steps in this book, your life can change too. This book is not a get rich quick scheme. It's a step-by-step process that you'll have to work hard at for years if you want to keep your revenue consistent.

THE BASICS

My dog training story

MY STORY STARTS IN 2007. I had two businesses in the bike industry and I was getting burned out. I wanted a change. I had two dogs at the time and was bound to regular business hours with my retail store. The businesses were both doing well, but I knew I had to make a change. Days were spent looking out the front door, daydreaming about being outside with my dogs. I was lucky that I could have my dogs at work with me all day, but I still wanted to be outside enjoying the sunshine. It felt a lot like middle school when I would watch the clock tick, tick, tick until it was time to get out of school and go have fun outside. So I did what any irresponsible man in his early twenties would have done, I closed both businesses and decided to take a year off, live off the proceeds and figure it out along the way. How naive.

NINE MONTHS WENT by like they were a week and I found myself praying to God. "Lord, I'm running out of money, I should probably start a business or something, what should I do?" Now, normally when I pray I don't feel like I get much direction, but I felt at that moment God was pushing me to follow my passion. "You're my son, and I love you, so do what makes you happy."

My fascination with dog training had started years before when I adopted my first dog, Phoenix, from a local shelter. He was totally out of control when I adopted him and I was in over my head. The shelter urged me to connect with a local trainer with over thirty years of experience. After intensely working with him for two months, Phoenix was still out of control. I would spend several hours a day working with him, but the methods were not right for Phoenix and his behavioral issues. I decided that I would have to fix things on my own because in those days dog trainers were in very short supply.

I spent the next year and a half connecting with other dog trainers over the internet, getting free advice, going to seminars and reading books. After two years of hard work, I finally had a dog I could trust. He went from pulling me down the road like an idiot to walking pleasantly on the leash. From chasing every small animal in the woods to being completely off leash reliable. I knew that I could help other people.

At the time I decided to go into dog training, I had eight years of entrepreneurial experience already so I thought it would be a breeze. Again... How naive.

I started meeting people at the park that would ask for my help, and I gladly helped them for free. I treated each client like they were paying me thousands of dollars. They were treated like kings and queens, often resulting in large tips, presents, and testimonials without me asking. I was changing people's lives, just because I wanted to help out. It felt amazing to help people and their best doggy friends.

As I looked around at the other local trainers, they were all offering inexpensive group classes as well as offering training by the hour. I did that for another year and a half with limited success. People would do a lesson or two, be happy with the changes and they would stop asking for more training. I was having a blast, but I was broke and had a big problem brewing. Acquiring new clients was a huge issue for me at the time. I was producing fast results for my clients and at the same time digging a hole for myself. I constantly needed to acquire more clients. Most clients were doing one to two lessons and I was only charging $40 per lesson, so at best I would make $40-$80 per client.

If you run the numbers, I had to convince a thousand people to train with me each year to make $60,000. After seeing the error of my ways, I knew I needed to make a change. Around the same time, I met a man by the name of Duke Ferguson who would forever change my life. He saw the fire in my eyes and decided to take me under his wing. His dog training skills were impressive, but his business skills were eye-opening. I was running out of cash and excuses at the same time. His business was doing great, so I decided to suck it up and go learn from someone wiser than myself.

I jumped in head first and spent the next five years learning from him. I more than doubled my salary in the first year and it kept growing. *The Formula* he taught me changed everything. Sure, I've refined it over the years, but it's like a vintage Swiss watch that gets passed down from generation to generation. A systematic way to market and sell dog training services. In this book, I'll distill that five-year education down for you into sizable chunks that you can integrate into your training business.

. . .

For me it was simple, I became a dog trainer so that I could support myself while doing something that I loved, and I was falling short on my promises. Now that I'm married and have a daughter, the stakes are a lot more tangible. This is not a game. I personally know many of the top dog trainers in the world and I will tell you this, most of them are living paycheck to paycheck. They focus on their dog skills and ignore the things that are actually going to move the needle. I'm not suggesting that the only thing dog trainers should focus on is the business while leaving their training skills to rust. That's precisely the opposite of what I'm suggesting.

The better your business is doing, the more money you'll have to invest in seminars, conferences, shadowing programs, DVDs, and other forms of ongoing education. It's extremely hard to focus on your dog training skills when you don't know where your next meal is going to come from. Trust me, I know from experience.

When to take the leap?

Mike jumped in head first like I did and we both were ill-prepared. We think that our dog training abilities will pay the bills, but they rarely do. If people don't know about you, how can they hire you? If you don't have proper programs at different price points, you'll alienate the majority of people who do hear about your business. Mike was sure that his business would take off when he had time to devote to it. He was working a full-time job that he hated, and he had convinced himself that if he had ultimate control of his days, he would have more clients than he could handle. My story was not much different. I had all the time in the world, but I had convinced myself that my previous business experience would be a significant asset in starting on this new path. Neither of us were prepared for what lay ahead.

For Mike, it became apparent pretty quickly that he was in trouble.

His clients were few and far between, and he was honest with me by telling me that he didn't like working with people. We both jumped the gun and should have created something special that was running smoothly before putting all of our eggs in one basket. I had a leg up on Mike because I like people, but my inability to explore different business models was holding me back at the time. Mike's growth was being stifled by his lack of people skills. He had some basic dog training programs, but no one had heard about his business, and he was not communicating the value he could provide to potential clients.

So WHEN SHOULD you make the leap to full time? When your business has made a significant profit every month for at least six months in a row and the business is making as much money as you are making at your full-time job. Having something to fall back on is not a bad thing and it can take a lot of pressure off of you. Sure, you'll be working insane hours for that period, but that tends to be the way good businesses are born. Replace your income before you go all in.

BUSINESS DEDUCTIONS, *zoning, insurance, contracts, and legal entities*

BUSINESS DEDUCTIONS

Always keep all of your receipts from things such as office supplies, dog equipment, and leashes so that you can claim the expenses at the end of the year. When you own a business, your profit is taxed. However, if you have receipts for normal business needs, you can submit those to decrease your profit at the end of the year which will decrease the amount of tax you owe the government.

HERE IS a list of some of the expenses that you can claim:

. . .

- Office supplies

- Collars and leashes

- Cleaning supplies

- Shipping and freight

- Your home office and utilities

- Car expenses

- Business insurance

- Charitable giving

- Clothing and footwear for work (with business logos)

Home office deductions are hard to calculate. Be sure to keep all of your heating/cooling costs, repairs, snow removal, mortgage statements or rent receipts for your home office or facility. My accountant is incredible at figuring out these deductions, and I would highly suggest you find a professional to evaluate how much you should be claiming as a deduction. I have a home and facility on the same property, so the lines are even fuzzier, but I'm able to deduct a large portion of my mortgage and expenses.

. . .

HERE'S where things get a little tricky. Can you deduct every expense for every one of your dogs? Some say yes, but I've heard from accountants in both Canada and the USA and the answer is almost never the answer you'll want to hear. If you purchase or adopt a dog for the specific purpose of using them as a demonstration dog in your business and purchase or adopt after starting your business, you can deduct your dog's dog food, grooming, and vet care. There is one way around this issue; if you change your business structure from a sole proprietorship to a corporation, you can put your dog's ownership into your company, and they are then legally seen as assets of the business.

IN MY CASE, one of my dogs was purchased just months before I legally opened up my business and so I'm not able to claim his expenses as a business expense. He's seen as a pet dog even though I use him daily as a demonstration dog for my business. One of my other dogs was purchased specifically as a demonstration dog after I opened my business so I'm able to deduct her expenses without issue. I even included her sale receipt as a business expense.

I KNOW plenty of dog trainers that claim 100% of everything for each of their dogs and some of them are in danger of a significant penalty if they are caught by the IRS or CRA. I follow this model because it's the safe bet, if you decide not to follow this model, you could be putting your business in a questionable position. When in doubt, call the IRS or CRA and ask them how to proceed.

CAR EXPENSES ARE a little more cut and dry, but there are a few ways you can approach them. Each trip can be marked down as personal or business with the starting and ending miles/kilometers from each trip. If you think this is too tedious, you can use plenty of smartphone apps for this task. I polled dog trainers to find out what app they use to track mileage and MileIQ was the clear winner. If you don't record your mileage and are audited, you could have issues, so please record your mileage in case you need to defend your deductions at a later time. Like a home office, a portion of your fuel, payments, and repairs can be claimed.

IF YOU DO free work for registered dog rescues or shelters, they can give you a receipt that suggests the price of the work you've donated and that can be deducted from your taxes! This is a great way to give back and get a tax break at the end of the year.

Legal Entities

Mike tried to ignore this part, and he's lucky that his local government didn't find out about his lack of permits before I forced him to comply with local laws. It can seem like an afterthought for some, but it won't be fun if you get caught before you can make things right. Please be diligent about this section and seek the proper industry professionals that you'll need to comply with the laws that apply to you and your business. Being in compliance with your federal and state/provincial business departments is not something you should avoid.

DETERMINING the type of business you will legally set up is essential. Here are the three main options you'll want to entertain.

A SOLE PROPRIETORSHIP (USA and Canada) is the most common way to set up a business in both Canada and the USA. It's the cheapest to start and to file. However, it doesn't offer any protection in the case of a legal battle. Essentially, you are the business, and if someone sues you, he or she could potentially take your assets including your car and home.

. . .

LLC (only available in the USA) is a very common way for trainers to be registered in the USA. The filing costs are reasonable. However, it provides good coverage in the case of a legal battle because it separates your personal assets from your business assets. Registering as an LLC is typically the best option for dog trainers, and it allows for a lower tax rate in most cases.

CORPORATIONS (USA and Canada) including C-Corp's and S-Corp's provide good liability coverage like the LLC. They are more costly to start and file, however, they can be a great option if your income is substantial as they offer lower tax rates as opposed to a sole proprietorship.

JUSTIN'S CASE STUDY:

Justin owns a dog training/boarding company in Texas and here's how he legally started his business.

1: He chose a business name.

2: He chose to be a for-profit business, not a non-profit.

3: He got a tax ID (online IRS). Be sure not to misplace this document!

4: He decided to file as an LLC.

5: He opened a DBA (designated business bank account).

6: He got his local county permits.

7: He got business insurance.

8: He applied for an employer identification number. (Only needed if you have employees.)

REGISTERING IN CANADA.

1: Contact the registry of joints and stocks in your province to do a business name search.

2: Pick your business name and register it with your province.

3: Determine if you will be a sole proprietor or corporation.
4: Choose to be a for-profit business, not a non-profit.
5: Register your business with the registry of joints and stocks.

You're required to submit your business sales each year and can include your tax deductions at the same time. If your business does more than $30,000 in sales per year, you must also contact CRA (Canada Revenue Agency) to get a GST/HST number. This will require you to charge HST on all sales within Canada. The HST can be filed to CRA on a monthly, quarterly, or yearly basis. For most small businesses, it's suggested to file HST on a quarterly basis.

When registering an LLC or Corporation, I would highly suggest contacting a lawyer who specializes in setting up businesses to help with the process of filing.

If you want to register an LLC or Corporation online, here are a few websites that can help you with that task:
https://www.incorporate.com/
https://www.gust.com
https://www.legalzoom.com/

Insurance

Insurance is critical for any business, and Mike also missed this step. You see Mike lives in the USA, a country of litigation. It's common for people to sue in the USA and in some ways it's part of the cultural fabric. Business insurance is the best investment you hopefully never have to use. Business liability insurance of one million dollars is the standard. However, if you plan to use your personal vehicle for business use (such as dropping off clients' dogs or picking up dog food), you'll want to ask your insurance broker if you also need a commercial vehicle insurance policy.

. . .

http://www.prolink.insure/ - Canada
http://www.dogtrainerinsurance.com/ - USA

Permits

You may be required to obtain permits for your business if you're planning on having clients come to your home for lessons or will be doing board and train clients in your home. The fewest permits are required for in-home dog trainers. The laws are different in each county and municipality so you'll have to do some research to determine the required permits. It's important also to understand how many dogs you are able to have on your property before needing to have a special kennel license.

Contracts

It's essential to have each and every one of your clients sign a contract. Signing a contract is an important way to decrease your liability as a dog trainer. When clients are signing the contract, make sure that they read it, and even have them initial the important parts like the sections on liability and refunds. Many contracts have been considered void because the clients claimed they didn't read the contract. You can take a look at a sample contract on our website and if you decide to use the sample contract, please have a lawyer look over the contract to make sure that it's acceptable for your business uses. For a reasonably priced lawyer, I highly recommend www.upwork.com

Market Research

I can't stress how important it is to find a market that's not being filled. Imagine you're a restaurateur. You love Italian food, so it seems only natural to open an Italian restaurant right? Your passion for Italian food may be met with fierce competition if you have an abundance of Italian restaurants in your area. Why not ask the people and resources who know best? Both Mike and I skipped this important step and our businesses suffered for it. We just assumed that we would figure it out along the way.

A GREAT FREE tool for picking a market is Google Adwords. They have a tool called the keyword planner tool that will allow you to search for keywords such as "dog training Binghamton NY," "obedience training Binghamton NY," "puppy training Binghamton NY," and "agility training Binghamton NY." This tool can show you how many monthly requests Google gets for the above keywords. Maybe you've planned to focus your business on agility training, but after doing the research, you find an incredibly low search volume with those keywords. If after doing more research, you find that puppy training is getting ten times the search volume, you may want to pivot your specialty into puppy training. The great thing is that once you've got these people as clients, you can often sell them other services like agility classes. Unfortunately, I've seen many of my friends disregard this keyword data and struggle for years to build a sustainable business because of their inability to change the direction of the business. Why bother providing a service if there is no interest in it?

I WAS fortunate in that I started getting calls from people asking me if I was able to work with aggressive dogs. I told about a dozen of them that I wasn't able to help them until I realized that right in front of my eyes was an incredible opportunity. Now I know what you're thinking. "Ted, you started working with these dogs even though you didn't have a lot of experience working with different aggressive dogs?" Well, not entirely. I told those clients I didn't have much experience, but I was willing to give it a try. So I started helping them for free and found that I had a great love for these dogs and a natural talent for helping aggressive dogs. After working with more and more, I started getting rolls of cash as a thank you and this was the moment I knew I could charge the clients money for working with these dogs.

. . .

THESE CLIENTS WERE SEARCHING high and low looking for someone to help them and they were met with trainers not willing to help, or trainers suggesting they euthanize their dog. I literally stumbled upon a greatly underserved market that had zero competition. Never forget to listen to what the market is telling you.

Another way to find an underserved market is to ask groomers and veterinarians. Meet with them and tell them of your desire to work with dogs. Ask them what types of training their clients needed. With that knowledge, you can go back to Google to do more research to see how much competition is associated with the data you've collected from the groomers and Veterinarians.

DON'T OVERLOOK online marketplaces like Craigslist and Kijiji. Post an advertisement asking dog owners what their needs are. In return, give them a free 30-minute phone consultation as a thank you. Collect your data and go back to Google to evaluate your competition. You'll want to make your best-educated guess as to the services that you should offer and at the same time, be ready to change direction as the market makes suggestions.

WHO'S YOUR TARGET MARKET? Contrary to popular belief, your target market is not everyone who owns a dog. If you don't know who your target is, you'll waste plenty of time and money marketing to the wrong people. I was shocked when I looked at my Google analytics. Google Analytics is a free tool that you can integrate into your website that tracks how users got to your website, how long they stayed on your website, and information like sex, computer operating system, and smartphone.

THE VAST MAJORITY of phone calls and emails I get are from women, so I always assumed my target had to be women. Sure the women were calling, but the overwhelming majority of people on my website were men between the ages of 35-44. Here I was marketing towards women for the last eight years and my target should have been men. Still to this day, I don't know the process, but I have a hunch that the men are looking for help and their partners are picking up the phone. Men can find it hard to ask for help; women, on the other hand, tend to have more humility when they feel they need help.

Today, my marketing is more focused on men, but I still aim to be approachable for my potential female clients. Numbers don't lie. In order to find that target, you'll need to get your feet wet. You'll want to work with people of all ages and genders. Many dog trainers find that their best clients are people like them. Humans tend to attract those they have things in common with. Finding your target client is essential in reducing your marketing budget and time spent acquiring new clients in addition to helping you find the clients who make teaching a pleasure.

Business Name

The business name you choose will affect your business long term, so take your time picking it now. If you've already started your business with a name that you don't like, you're stuck with it unless you want to change your name which will cost money to rebrand your website, print new business cards, and inform your clients and potential clients of the change. Changing your business name is almost always a bad decision.

Using play-on-words like Pawsative should be avoided because there are so many companies with those names already. Choose a name that's easy for people to remember. You could even use your city's name which could greatly help your business get found on Google. A name like Denver Dog Training is a great name because it tells the person what your company does and where you're located. Don't be afraid to kill two birds with one stone. Stay away from using K9 because the average dog owner doesn't know what K9 means. They probably think you train police dogs because they see K9 on police dog cars. Don't be afraid to stand out with your name, or you might just blend into the pack.

Learn how to train dogs.

You probably already know that the dog training industry is unregulated in North America. This means that anyone can print business cards and make the claim that they're a professional dog trainer. I'm not sure how I feel about the industry being unregulated. On one side, it makes it easy for people to get into dog training. On the other side, it makes it easier for people to train dogs who really shouldn't be working with dogs. There are dozens of paths to becoming a professional dog trainer. While this book is a great resource for would-be dog professionals, it leaves out a major part of the equation: the dog training. Let's discuss a few avenues for getting more knowledge before taking the step into the role of a professional. Let's examine the two most popular ways that people choose when becoming a dog trainer.

1: You can go to school to learn how to become a professional dog trainer. Some of these schools are better than others, so please do your own research.

Force-free methods:
  Jean Donaldson Academy for Dog Trainers- USA
  Karen Pryor Academy- USA

Balanced methods:
  Tom Rose School for Dog Trainers- USA
  The Michael Ellis School for Dog Trainers- USA
  Starmark Academy- USA
  Tarheel Canine- USA

National K9- USA
That's My Dog- USA
Canada West Canine Center- Canada

Dog training schools are a great benefit to the aspiring dog trainer because they allow for a combination of theory-based learning and practical experience. While any of these schools would be a great option, please keep in mind that most dog training schools are not great at providing students with two of the most important skills you'll need to be successful as a self-employed dog trainer. Dog training schools are not diligent at teaching students the business of dog training and how to work successfully with clients. If you attend any of these schools, please be earnest in your efforts to learn client coaching skills and how to sell your dog training service.

2. The self-taught model is a luxury that most industries don't have and it's the model that both Mike and I used when entering into the industry. If you want to be a medical doctor, get ready for med-school because it's your only option. Dog trainers have the great benefit of being able to learn over time, on their own time.

Here's how I did it. When flirting with the idea of becoming a dog trainer, I already had years of experience training my own dogs, as well as dogs who belonged to friends of mine. I was eating and breathing dog training at the time. At the time, drug detection and personal protection were my two favorite things to fool around with. After doing some research, I came to the conclusion that there was essentially no market for clients who wanted to invest in training such things, so I switched gears towards the pet dog market.

It was clear to me that I needed much more experience with different breeds and behavioral issues before I could confidently ask people to pay me. That was fine with me as I began to train dogs for free. Meeting people in the park, I would often have people comment on my dogs' good behavior and focus. This prompted me to ask them if they wanted help with their own dogs for free and most people were enthused by the proposition. So that's what I did. I trained dogs for free for about a year, asking only for a testimonial in return. After training many dogs for free, I had testimonials to aid me as I prepared to pick a business name and make a website for my business.

THE NEXT THING I did was invest in a correspondence course. The course structure was great; they sent me books and training manuals in the mail. Students were to film themselves training dogs and send in the video footage for critique. When I felt I had a good grasp on the science behind dog training and some practical skills, I started attending dog training seminars to develop a more inclusive perspective on the different tools and techniques available. Armed with dog training experience, testimonials and the theory of training, I was ready to build a website and print business cards so that I could go to the market.

THERE ARE dozens of different ways you can make the transition; feel free to be creative and never underestimate the power of finding a great mentor which was something I did early in my business and thank God for that. For the first year and a half, I was completely on my own, and it wasn't until I was struggling that I linked up with Duke Ferguson. My training skills were great, I was great with the dogs and owners, but I couldn't figure out a way to make a sustainable business out of what I had created. As mentioned before, I was stuck because I was charging per hour and that required me to acquire multiple clients a day if I wanted to make a reasonable income from my business. It was not even close to sustainable.

MIKE'S EDUCATION before dog training was very limited. He had read some books, been to a few seminars and had trained his own dogs. His dog training skills were adequate, but what he really needed was more practice. For every five clients he would sign up, one would really challenge his training abilities. This is not always something to be concerned about in the first few years and it's somewhat normal if you're working with dogs with aggression, anxiety, or severe behavioral problems.

IF YOU FIND yourself feeling inadequate as a trainer in the first few years, that's okay. Even trainers who go to an extensive dog training school will have moments of feeling inadequate. About a decade later, I still get dogs that I find hard to figure out, so don't sweat it. Time and repetition will help, and be open to learning from others.

If you don't feel ready, you can train more dogs for free, or train at a fee but extend a full money-back guarantee if the client is not 100% happy with the results or service. Part of dog training is learned on the job, and that's okay, just make sure that people are happy with the way things are progressing and that they know you don't have hundreds or thousands of dogs trained yet. Honesty is critical.

ACCESS your free business resources here: http://www.tedsbooks.com/trainer-docs

PICKING THE RIGHT BUSINESS MODELS

Introduction to business models
A business model is a framework that allows a business to make money. In this chapter, we'll explore some of the most popular business models in the world of dog training and discuss some of the positives and negatives associated with each model. You don't need to have all of the answers, but you do need to be willing to change course if the market is not interested in what you're offering. When starting our businesses, both Mike and I had insufficient business models.

6 SAMPLE BUSINESS models

Years ago, I went to a group class with my first dog, Phoenix. Maybe it was wrong of me to assume we would work on leash walking, but I did. Seven of the eight weeks went by and right at the very end of the last session we spent a few minutes learning about leash walking. We were instructed to lure our dogs with a treat when we walked to prompt attention from our dogs. Each week, I was fifteen minutes early and I watched each week as every dog in the class came out of the car and pulled the owner into the class.

. . .

WHEN EACH CLASS WAS DONE, the same thing would happen, every dog would pull their owners out of the class on the way to the car. The program seemed extremely counter-productive. Why were we learning basic commands in a church basement when the students actually needed to learn how to walk their dogs on a loose leash? Leash walking seemed like an afterthought. At the end of the last session, I talked with the head trainer who didn't have any specific classes for such issues and so I left defeated.

HE WAS nice enough to give me a few additional tips before leaving the class. However, they proved fruitless when I practiced at home on my own. After thirty years of training dogs, this trainer had still not changed his business model to include what his clients actually wanted and needed to learn. Years later, his lack of desire to change made it incredibly easy to figure out what type of services I would provide in my new training business. So I started by asking my clients what they wanted to learn. It seems so simple, but many trainers miss this huge opportunity even after decades in the dog training industry. Never underestimate the flood of positive word of mouth advertising you can gain by teaching clients what they want to learn. If they are having issues with their dogs, help them fix the issues. If they want to learn specific obedience commands, great! Give the customer what they want.

IT'S easy to determine what your clients want; you just have to ask them. Recently I was teaching a group of dog trainers in an online mastermind course and I asked each of them to stop the lesson to go get their client evaluation forms. I had each of them look through their evaluation forms from their past clients and present their findings to the group. It didn't surprise me to watch every one of these trainers say the exact same things.

THEIR CLIENTS WANTED their dogs to stop pulling on the leash, stop jumping up on people and stop barking. Many also wanted their dogs to come when called. After the exercise, several of the trainers messaged me to say that they had decided to completely change how they run their businesses. They were teaching dogs to do things that people didn't care about and it can only be assumed that people will not consistently practice things that they don't care about. Having a predetermined curriculum is usually only good for group training classes. Private training should always be a-la-carte. Again, give your customers what they want.

A BUSINESS MODEL is a structure behind how your business makes money. Each product or service that you can sell will have a business model and it's ok to have different business models within your company. Take Netflix, for example. They sell monthly subscriptions for customers to enjoy entertainment. Facebook offers a free service but makes money by selling ads to its advertising partners. Your business will sell dog training services, but how you sell those services is incredibly important.

NOT ALL BUSINESS models are created equally, so please examine how your products and services will make money or you might run into the problem I faced early on with acquiring new customers. Your low-priced options need to be in a group class setting so that you can have eight to twelve clients in each class. This will free up a lot of your time. Your private training must be much more expensive because of its unsustainable model. As you will learn in this chapter, I've found a sweet spot by integrating both private and group classes.

BUSINESS MODEL 1: Private training

Private training has a lot of positives attached to it. It's great to be one-on-one with a client and their dog. You can accomplish much more and the client's retention of the information will be much greater than with group training alone. In private lessons, you'll be able to focus on the client and the dog or dogs you're training. In-home options are also available in this model which is something clients find incredibly compelling. Every day, I have people call me who are fed up with group classes. They are seeking a more personal experience.

SOME PEOPLE FEEL ALIENATED by group classes. They feel that their dog can't focus on the task at hand because of all the other dogs and people. Another reason that private lessons are in such high demand is their innate ability to be flexible. For example, in a group class environment, if one or two students have to miss lesson three because of work obligations, they are going to be lost when lesson four comes.

IF YOU OFFER PRIVATE SESSIONS, I recommend that you only allow your clients to buy them in packages. Three sessions should be the minimum package you provide. Why? If you sell private lessons, you'll always be stuck in a race to acquire more clients. You'll be running around like a chicken with its head cut off, trying to get more clients because your clients will do one session, get some good results and not call you back. The model is not sustainable. Given the option, most people will only put in the effort to make their dog 20% better unless they have someone keeping them accountable. Also, bear in mind that if a client purchases a package of sessions, a few other things will happen. At the end of each lesson, you'll book them for the next lesson. This alone has huge psychological implications spurring them on to do the homework before the next session.

PEOPLE FEEL the need to get what they paid for. This will aid you in producing clients who do the work you ask them to do. These clients will be more diligent about taking things seriously and will be more likely to do the homework. If you do sell packages, you also have the option of gamification. Gamification is the process of incentivizing people to achieve a level of success with a reward like a certificate. It may seem counterintuitive to stick to your guns on this model, but you'll have to take my word for it.

OFFERING in-home lessons to clients is a great way to start off your business. Like everything we discuss in this book, in-home lessons have positives and negatives associated with them. Many use this model in the early days because it doesn't require the financial investment of having a training facility. Every day, I see in-home dog trainers that don't utilize the in-home training benefits in their marketing and website. When I bought my property and started having clients come to my facility, I lost clients because potential clients wanted an in-home trainer.

IF I COULD GIVE myself advice ten years ago, I would drill in the importance of emphasizing that I was an in-home dog trainer. Don't miss this free opportunity. It's easy to start implementing, all you need is a car. People love the idea that their trainer will be coming to their home to help them. A common misconception among dog owners is that if their dog is not trained at their home, their dogs will only respond in the specific training environment where the dog was trained.

LIKE ANY BUSINESS MODEL, private lessons are not without issues. Clients don't take your safety as seriously as they would if they were coming onto your property. There is a gap between how people act when you are in their home and when they bring their dog to your property. This situation requires special attention from the trainer. You need to communicate well with the potential client about what they should do before you come over to their house. An example of this would be a client who allows their dogs to bark and jump at the door when you are at the front door waiting to come in. All the while they say, "He's ok, he's just excited, he'll be fine."

. . .

IF ONLY I had a nickel for each of the scars on my friends' arms who listened to these statements without listening to their gut. If you're going to go to people's homes every day and don't have systems set up to keep yourself safe, you will be bitten; it's not a matter of if, but when. When speaking with the client over the phone, ask them to have the dog in the home when you come to meet, if they have a martingale collar, it can be attached to a leash, and they must be holding the leash. It's essential to properly communicate your expectations with potential clients so that they can be prepared before meeting you.

ASKING them to have a leash and collar on their dog is not enough. You will need to ask them to have either a martingale collar or a tightly fitted collar on the dog so that they can't slip out of the collar. I've seen dogs slip out of collars far too many times; I've even seen dogs get out of harnesses. Always have an extra slip leash on hand in case you get to the home and find the dog is wearing a collar that resembles a necklace.

MEN DON'T TYPICALLY THINK ABOUT personal safety when going to a client's home but I know hundreds of female dog trainers who do. Regardless of your gender, you should make your safety a priority. A great app available for Android and Apple is called BSafe. BSafe will allow you to set estimated arrival and departure times in the app as well as a location. So here's how it would work for a dog trainer. You program your start time, ending time, and location of the clients home into the app. If you and your phone haven't left the designated location by the pre-specified session ending time, the app uses GPS to automatically send an alert to one of your chosen emergency contacts with your location information. www.getbsafe.com

BUSINESS MODEL 2: *Board and trains*
   A board and train is the process of taking a dog in for training and

then training the clients to keep the same results and routine. Plenty of trainers love this option because it allows them to focus on dog training and not teaching the client. It's true that if you do a great job of training the dog, the process of training the owner is typically easier. However, this model has many potential drawbacks. Many trainers believe that because they can charge thousands of dollars for a board and train program, that this is the most profitable business model. It's not. I've run the numbers, and even at $4,000 per board and train, it was still more profitable for me to train the clients one on one. How can this be?

WHEN YOU FACTOR in the hours you'll invest in feeding, training, and exercising the dog, that big sale doesn't look as appetizing. Factor in the additional insurance costs, sleepless nights, stress that your personal dogs will endure and disagreements with your spouse, it looks even less appetizing. Clearly, I'm not exactly enthusiastic about board and trains, but you have to keep in mind that I did them for many years. I know what it did to my personal life, financial life, and my dogs' lives.

THE MAJORITY of the trainers I know who offer this service struggle pretty consistently with unhappy clients. Board and trains are often sold as the easy option and that's only partially true. The trainer does the up-front training, but the client will still have to change the way they live to ensure that the results stick. Don't forget that the client also needs to be taught the methods you used and so you are still responsible for training the client. When you market this service, it's okay to market it as a short-term timesaver, but be sure to properly set expectations about how much the client will need to change and for how long in order to see lasting results.

EACH CLIENT SHOULD HAVE training before, during, and after the board and train and should have detailed step-by-step written homework for them to follow. In addition, it will be of great benefit to offer free drop-in group classes for ongoing support. Board and trains are a great way to ensure the dog will get consistent training every day. Many trainers believe it's the only way to work with dogs with severe behavioral problems or a history of aggression. I've not found that to be the case at all. Just because I'm not enthusiastic about this business model, it doesn't mean that you should avoid board and trains. Test it out, see if you like it. You can always stop providing them if you feel the need.

BUSINESS MODEL 3: *Group classes*

A traditional group class has one or more trainers who are helping guide clients and dogs through a predetermined curriculum. These classes often focus on puppy training or basic obedience. Due to the nature of group classes, the curriculum must be determined in advance before starting the classes. I know several trainers who love the group classes they hold because they are able to work with a lot of dogs very quickly. This business model is a great solution for offering a lower priced training option for clients who are not prepared to make a significant financial investment into dog training.

GROUP CLASSES CAN ALSO HAVE some negatives in that they do not serve clients who need extra attention well. You'll want to put some systems into your business to make it easy for customers to get the class information and register on your website. Manually taking payments and booking for group classes can quickly become an overwhelming burden. A free online resource that I use in such cases is www.bigcartel.com. Bigcartel is a free online store website that will allow you to make a simple online store with class information and the ability to purchase a class. You'll need a Paypal account to accept payments, but don't worry because Payal is free and allows your customers to pay with any major credit card.

. . .

BUSINESS MODEL 4: *Private / Group*

The private / group training model is hands down my favorite model. Within this business model, you sell clients a combination of private training that transitions into group classes. Personally, I offer four private lessons and then twelve months of free group classes. It's a flexible model so be sure to play around as you see fit for your business. Clients love this model because they get one on one training with me in a low distraction environment and also have the opportunity to work around more distractions when they transition into group classes. The drop-in group classes are a great way to incentivize your clients to stay on top of training. Clients are much more likely to stay consistent with the training they learned in the private lessons because they can come to the group classes as their schedules allow at no extra charge.

IN THIS MODEL, I don't have a predetermined curriculum. I ask the clients what they want to learn and then start. My drop-in group classes are a revolving program, each week one to two dogs integrate into the class. Each week as new dogs are coming in, other dogs are filtering out. You can also upsell these clients before they filter out after twelve months for another twelve months of group classes at an additional charge. The private / group business model has been proven to be the most profitable model by many trainers around the world. The clients are happy because they get as much training as they want and the trainer is happy because they have happy, successful clients who are keeping up with the training. Each week, we go for a group walk together, do obedience drills, and, if we have time, do socialization and address any specific issues that any client may be facing. The classes are one hour, and I hold them at a local park near my house every Saturday. Some counties/municipalities do not allow dog trainers to conduct business in local parks so please research any laws that pertain to your business.

BUSINESS MODEL 5: *Puppy training*

Anytime you can start a client young, it's a win-win for everyone involved. The majority of dog trainers hold puppy classes to promote socialization for young puppies. Puppy training is an easy sell to clients for a few reasons:

• Most dog owners feel that it's their responsibility to start their dog's life off with puppy classes.

• THEY KNOW that socialization is going to be significantly more difficult at an older age.

• PUPPY TRAINING IS TYPICALLY HELD in a group environment and so the classes can be inexpensive.

PUPPY TRAINING often gives your clients confidence that they have done everything they need to do for their puppies. 70% of dog owners receive puppy training in Canada and yet only 4% receive advanced level training. Why is that? It's an expectation problem. Dog owners are convinced that, after puppy training, their dog has all the obedience and socialization tools they will need to live a fulfilled life. While this can be the case with some dogs, more often it's not. If you decide to sell puppy training, you'll want to educate puppy owners on the benefits of continuing the training process as their dog develops.

A CASE STUDY WITH JENNA:

Jenna's a new dog trainer who's seen the potential in training puppies because three of her friends from high school got new puppies in the last year. After being asked a handful of times, she decides to take the plunge. She rents a local community hall for $30/hour and calls her friends. Things go swimmingly, it's a hit. It's been 6 weeks now, all the puppies are fourteen to eighteen weeks old and she thanks her friends as they leave the community hall after their last lesson.

She's proud of herself and clearly she did a great job with the puppies. She hopes her friends will call her as the puppies grow up and need additional training. Great job, Jenna! Jenna decides to do another class a few weeks later and puts up a flyer on Facebook. She gets a few calls but decides she'll have to cancel the class due to a lack of clients. She's discouraged. It's now been months and her friends haven't called her about their growing puppies. She decides that puppy training is a pain and goes back to offering private lessons by the hour.

A CASE STUDY WITH KARY:

Kary has a mentor who's got the dog business figured out. She sits down with her mentor as she gives her plenty of ideas how to structure her new puppy classes. She's got pages of notes and decides to go home and really dive into her options. She's done significant research into her competition, including what they are providing for puppy classes and she wants to do something completely different. She decides that she's going to offer an "all you can train" puppy class for puppies between the ages of eight and twenty-four weeks. Kary went to her local dog park and asked dog owners about their experience with taking their dogs to puppy classes when they were young. She hears a few different things.

- I LIKED ALLOWING my puppy to socialize, but I feel like we didn't really get much information or help with basic things like the puppy biting and jumping up.

- I LIKED ALLOWING my puppy to socialize with other puppies, but I found that only socializing with puppies was very limiting. What we really needed to learn was how to socialize our puppy with older dogs.

. . .

• I really liked the class, but it would have been nice to continue to connect with some of the dogs from the puppy class.

• The classes were great, but unexpected work commitments forced me to skip two classes and I felt overwhelmed the next week when we came back.

Kary got plenty of information to aid her in making her classes. Her classes will be "all you can train." She'll charge a higher amount than her local competitors because her classes allow for more training time and are more flexible. Her competition is charging between $99 and $139 for their classes. She's going to charge $189 with the hope that people will see the extra value she's adding to her classes.

Here are a few things she does to separate herself from her competition:
    • She charges a higher price, suggesting that she's providing more value

• She creates a 50% discounted option for local shelters and dog rescues

• She has weekly homework for her clients and even goes so far as to take short videos and upload them to YouTube to demonstrate the weekly homework clients will do. If her clients have to miss a session, they can still use the videos to keep up.

• She has two of her friends come in each week with their middle-aged dogs to help socialize the puppies with older dogs.

. . .

- SHE CREATES a weekly social group for the dogs at a local park and a Facebook page so her clients can keep in touch as their dogs mature. She only leads the group for a few months, then appoints a few clients to help run the socials.

- SHE'S sure to give clients written homework each week.

- HER CURRICULUM FOCUSES on what her clients want including basic puppy issues like puppy biting, jumping up, and pulling on the leash.

- SHE KNEW that things were going to get busy, so she proactively made her simple online store on www.bigcartel.com to help with booking new puppy clients online.

- KARY EDUCATED the clients each week about the importance of continuing with training. She's sure to give each client a flyer that illustrates the importance of continuing training at key points of development. You'll be pleased to hear that she has a specific training program for each of those developmental periods. She created the flyers for free on www.canva.com and had them printed locally. Vistaprint.com is a great, economical alternative to local printers.

- KARY MAKES MORE flyers to promote her referral program. She's giving away a $25 gift card to Starbucks to any of her clients who refer a friend to the puppy classes. It works; she gets three new puppies in the next week.

- SHE'S sure to email each of her clients three weeks after finishing the puppy classes asking for them to take a quick survey.

. . .

• KARY TRACKS when the canine birthdays are and sends birthday emails at six months and one year.

• MONTHS AGO, Kary contacted dog food companies, dog treat manufacturers, and dog toy companies and has arranged for boxes of free food samples, toys, and treats in exchange for Kary hanging a few banners in the community hall where she holds her classes. Her clients are ecstatic with the free stuff!

JENNA'S CASE study was bland and traditional, and that's why it didn't prove to be extremely fruitful. Kary, on the other hand, did the research, under-promised and over-delivered. Her clients will tell their friends because her puppy class is remarkable. "Remarkable doesn't mean remarkable to you. It means remarkable to me. Am I going to make a remark about it? If not, then you're average, and average is for losers." - Seth Godin.

BUSINESS MODEL 6: Day school training
   Developing a consistent revenue source will help your business get through the inevitable ups and downs. Think of day school training like enriched doggy daycare. Clients drop off their dogs in the morning before work and come and pick them up after work. During the day, they play with the trainer's dogs, go out for hikes, take naps, and do some training with the trainer. The dogs go home each day tired from a day of exercise and learning and the clients are happy to have a tired dog whose training was being enhanced while they were at work.

DAY SCHOOL TRAINING is often a great option for busy clients who want to pay you to continue their dog's obedience training after they have worked with you as a client. Socialization, not being home alone, ongoing training, what's not to love? Trainers can do this training from their homes, without the need for a large facility, if they want to keep monthly costs down.

Free Evaluations

You're about to learn about a secret weapon that many of the most financially successful dog trainers in the world use: the free evaluation. There are plenty who would cry out blasphemy at the notion. I've heard all of the arguments about why offering anything for free in dog training is a terrible idea. I'll list a few:

• I'm going to lose time I can't get back, what if they don't sign up?

• They won't take you seriously if you offer something for free.

• Free attracts the wrong type of people.

• I'm not driving to them for free' that's preposterous. I'm losing time and having to pay for gas.

Some call them assessments, some demonstrations, others call them evaluations, but the terminology doesn't matter because it's just a meeting for you to show potential clients that you're the right gal or guy for the job. Sure, you can charge for evaluations, and this is a reasonable option. The going rate for evaluations is to charge about $80 and then discount $80 from the potential client's program rate if they sign up at the evaluation. This simple step helps ensure you weed out some of the people who are not serious and also incentivizes them to save $80. This little tweak actually works. This is a great option if you're worried about some of the concerns listed above.

Regardless of whether you charge people for the evaluation, you're going to get no-shows from time to time and people who are not a good fit and that's ok. When I was an in-home trainer, I only had two potential clients cancel the free evaluation over all the years I had done them. When I got my facility, that number increased from .5% to about 5%. That's a cost of doing business. Most trainers put aside forty-five minutes for an evaluation on average. Because I'm selling only high ticket programs that require a large investment I usually spent about an hour and fifteen minutes with potential clients.

It's important to do your best to have clients who are in a relationship to bring their spouse. I can't tell you how many times I've seen a potential client come without a spouse, be completely sold, and then email me the next day saying that their spouse thought they shouldn't sign up. It's now mandatory that the spouse comes to the evaluation.

WHETHER YOU MEET in person or chat over the phone, your goal for the evaluation is to show your potential client that you are a confident, competent trainer whose goal is to teach without judgment. Mike had never tried free evaluations and was convinced that they were a waste of time and gas money. He was unwilling to try new things, and his business was suffering because of his preconceived notions. In reality, he was struggling with fear. Fear that people would say no. Fear that he would invest several hours into a potential client only to have them be not interested. After our four hour discussion over the phone, I had persuaded him to give them a try and it was the single biggest change he made that actually turned into income.

MIKE BELIEVED that the purpose of his website was to educate potential clients about the tools and techniques that he uses. His prices were posted on his website and were driving the small number of visitors away because they didn't have context. You see, websites are amazing at some things, but building trust and building rapport are not among them. I told Mike that I had run the numbers. Allowing my website to sell the clients resulted in a remarkably low amount of sales. Free phone evaluations helped increase the likelihood of a sale, but it was not even a question when looking at the numbers for free in-person evaluations. I had a 75% sales rate with in-person evaluations. My numbers for website conversions were more like 5%, and phone evaluations were about 25%.

So you have to ask yourself, what is it about a free in-person evaluation that drastically increases the potential of a sale? I think I know the answer. It's called the law of reciprocity. This law says that when you give to others, most will feel obligated to reciprocate your benevolence. I've asked clients why they signed up and here are a few of the reasons I get consistently.

- Other trainers weren't willing to meet, but you were, and we didn't want to make such a big decision for our family without at least meeting a potential trainer.

- WHEN WE MET, we could tell that you were very knowledgeable and confident that you could help our dog.

- WE LIKED YOUR PERSONALITY; you weren't judgemental.

- YOU WORKED with our dog for ten minutes and clearly had focus and control over him in that time.

- YOU DIDN'T BEAT around the bush, you were very forthcoming about what you expected from your clients, and we liked knowing where we stood.

- YOU OFFERED to refer us to other trainers if we didn't want to sign up, which was a huge deal for us because it showed us how much you actually wanted us to get the right help even if it didn't put money in your pocket.

I DON'T KNOW what the right answer is for you, but I would suggest that you test these three options and do what's best for your business. Don't underestimate the power of the free evaluation. For three out of ten, it will be a waste of time, but don't think of it that way, think of it as an investment in your education. If you do things right, even if the client doesn't sign up, they will refer people to you.

DON'T LIKE SELLING? Me either! I hate it. I usually un-sell people. We start by going through my client evaluation form. I ask them questions and make notes. I spend extra time allowing them to vent if they need to. We talk about what they want their dog to be like after training and then I work with their dog for a few minutes to show them that I'm not all talk and no action. Next, we discuss the methods and tools that I use and why I think they would benefit their dog's life. The price quote comes last.

IT'S NOT unusual that the client is confused about why their dog is acting the way that they are and so I'm sure to try and give some insight. I then give them a quote and assure them that I can help them reach their training goals. Don't forget that last part, I still forget to do this, but it's a critical part of the trust building component of the evaluation. If you can't help them and don't want to try, be honest with them and refer them to someone who can.

IT'S ALWAYS nice if you can have multiple tiers of training programs so that they can have several training options at different prices. Every client is informed that I don't have refunds of any kind. If they ask me when they can start, I will sign them up on the spot but if they suggest they need to go home and talk about it I don't push for the sale. I tell them to take all the time they need and thank them for coming. They leave with a price quote that I fill out for them. When they leave they know roughly how long the training process is going to take, the tools and techniques I would use and how much time they're expected to invest in ongoing training. Having this detailed plan is essential for clients to know if they want to buy into my business or not.

FOR AN EVALUATION FORM you can use in your business, go to: http://www.tedsbooks.com/trainer-docs

DROP-IN GROUP CLASSES

Another key element of *The Formula,* drop-in group classes, are an incredible game changer for the trainers that utilize them. As an add-on to private training and board and train programs, I always include unlimited drop-in group classes as part of the service. Initially, I was skeptical of the idea because it would be an ongoing weekly commitment that I would have to provide for years to come. Just weeks into implementing the classes, I was starting to understand why offering these classes had such a massive effect on my increasing sales. Charging a client $1,000 for a training program with four to six private lessons is almost impossible because they do the math. Charging them $1,000 for a year of training makes much more sense.

THE FORMULA AT ITS BEST.

As taught to me, *The Formula* was simple but required me to change 90% of how I ran my failing dog training business. I'm so glad I made the changes because if I hadn't, I would be living a much different life than I am now. Start by driving referrals from veterinarians to get the phone ringing, then book the potential client for a free evaluation. In the free evaluation, educate the potential client about the tools and techniques that you use. Be sure to remind them multiple times that you can help them. Work with their dog for five to ten minutes and then give them a few program options and prices. The prices are not listed on the website; they are given to the client right at the end of the evaluation.

TRAIN the client and their dog in private lessons or board and train and then transition them into free drop-in group classes to ensure that the training does not deteriorate. Always do an incredible job and drive the referral for more clients. Under-promise and over-deliver. While my clients pay thousands of dollars for my service I still have them say it was the best money they ever spent. This is the secret sauce that has helped thousands of dog trainers around the world go from struggling to successful. The majority of dog training franchises are built on this model because it can and has been replicated by trainers all around the world.

HOW MUCH TO CHARGE FOR *your services*

In general, I suggest that trainers should charge more than most of their competition. Potential clients will automatically assume that your service is higher quality because of your higher price. Is premium gasoline actually better gas? I don't know, but I do know it costs more and it's called premium, so my brain assumes that it is. This is a natural pricing bias that all people have. You need to over-deliver on your service with every client and position your business as a high-quality brand. A dog trainer's prices can tell me a lot about how much confidence the trainer has.

WHAT ARE YOU AFRAID OF? Someone saying no? That's part of owning a business. Even if you offer free training, people can still say no, so don't sweat the rejection. The fear is just a mind game. I've helped plenty of people for free over the years and time and time again they are less consistent than my clients who pay full price. So even if you offer free or low-priced training, you may actually deal with more rejection than if you offer a premium service.

. . .

IF YOU MAKE a business everyone likes, you'll make a business no one loves!

You can't be everything for everyone! The amount that a client pays you is directly linked to how much effort they will put into the training process. Every year, my prices increase and every year I get better, more committed clients. Is that a coincidence? People take seriously what they pay dearly for.

CREATE three to four programs at different price points. Start at a lower rate and increase the rate as you get busier. You'll know when to stop increasing the price when you get ten no's in a row! I suggest having a low-priced option, a medium option and a high-priced option for your clients to choose from. Don't give clients too many options to choose between. All businesses should over-deliver on promises regardless of the price of the product or service they're selling. If you find yourself in a competitive battle, increase your value, don't lower your price.

IF YOU'RE a slacker and just want to provide a reasonable service, then charge a reasonable rate, but don't for a moment expect people to take time out of their day to to tell people about your business unless you're remarkable. The world is saturated with average businesses. Go above and beyond and reap the benefits through a cascade of positive word-of-mouth referrals. Be an amazing movie; you know the one you went to see last month that was so incredible that you told thirty people about it. Be that movie.

IF YOUR COMPETITION is charging next to nothing, don't take a cue from them. You'll need to reinvent the wheel. When I started, I was charging $40 per session. After learning *The Formula*, I created a program that was a hit at $750 a program. After about six months, I was so busy that I couldn't take any more clients, so I started increasing the price in $100 increments. I found that the sweet spot was around $1,250. Any price over that and I would decrease my signature rate; as I started testing into the $1,500 to $2,000 territory. I still had people sign up but not as many. Taking that leap from $40 per session to $750 a program was hard for me to do, but I knew how much extra value I was providing for the clients and their dogs.

IF YOU WERE STRUGGLING with your dog how much money would you pay to have someone completely change your life? I can remember so many times I felt defeated with Phoenix and would have gladly paid someone $2,000 or more if they could have helped us. Don't underestimate the power you hold to change someone's life forever.

MANGO DOGS IS GROWING and we'll help you get up to speed on your dog training skills, handle all of your marketing and you'll be part of our team. For more information go to: www.mangodogs.com/join

FIND THE CLIENTS

Mike's idea of marketing was sitting by the phone and waiting for it to ring. Unfortunately, that's not how it works. I was able to give him plenty of actionable ideas that were able to fix one of his largest issues, which was not having enough clients. There are ultimately two major ways to get new clients. Word-of-mouth referrals and internet referrals.

Social media

This is a touchy subject because so many people like to live private lives, and I can sympathize with that. In 2018, there are still millions of businesses that are not on social media who are doing hundreds of thousands or millions of dollars of revenue each year without much of an online presence. I don't think it's essential to be on social media, but I do typically suggest that having a presence is certainly better than not having one. It's likely that your competition has a social media presence so you may be missing out on some opportunities if you choose not to.

Entire books could be written on all of the different platforms and what they are used for, so I'm not going to tackle that huge topic. Here's the thing that you need to know about social media. You can't be everywhere and you shouldn't be everywhere. Figure out what your strengths are, make a decision, and be consistent at providing value to your viewers. If you love doing video and have a natural talent for it, get on YouTube! If you love writing, start a blog.

I'VE HAD great success with Facebook over the years, and it's been a great investment for the time I've devoted to it. Not only does Facebook have the most users, but it's also a place where people do research about companies because businesses are able to have groups and pages. If you decide to have a Facebook page, there are plenty of great YouTube video tutorials online to show you how to personalize your business Facebook page.

TO REALLY THRIVE ON FACEBOOK, you'll need to be consistent. Post interesting dog-related ideas, blogs, photos and how to videos. I suggest posting at least once a week but twice a week is ideal. Don't know what to post? Here are a few ideas on things that I've seen produce good engagement.

• ASK your followers to post the cutest photo that they have ever taken of their dog.

• ASK your followers what things make their dogs special.

• ANSWER FREQUENTLY ASKED questions on your Facebook that you get every day in your training business.

• POST INFORMATION that may be pertinent to dog owners in your area like new dog-related laws, dramatic increases in a dog-related disease and dog-friendly places locally that your followers can take their dogs.

THE IDEA IS to leverage people's desire to connect and talk about something or someone they love. Put some time into coming up with your posts and don't forget to provide value for the followers. The most effective social media pages and personalities in the dog training world constantly help and entertain their followers. If you invest a little, you'll get a little back. If social media is all about you, your followers will lose interest.

NOBODY WANTS to talk about social media skill, patience, and passion. Every social media guru in the world will urge you to get onto most of these platforms but they never talk about your ability or the timeline. These followings are not built overnight. It takes years of consistent dedication to make a significant impact on your business, so you better love the social media platform that you have focused on or else you'll quit before things can grow.

IF YOU'RE terrible on camera, don't feel pressured into doing video because it will look terrible. Every day I see trainers posting mediocre videos because they were told they had to be an online guru and it's disingenuous. If you've been posting daily for twelve months and you can't get a like from anyone but your mother, you're wasting your time. Focus on your strengths. Is blogging your thing? Is meeting people at a dog park your thing? Find your thing and double down.

WEBSITES:
If you don't have a website, you'll want to make one or have someone make one for you. I took a keen interest in making websites in high school and made my first website eighteen years ago. Back in

2000, unless you could make your own website, they were very expensive. Fast forward eighteen years and it's simple and inexpensive to get your own website. You don't need to know how to code. Most website building platforms are drag and drop these days which means that you can choose the elements you want and just click one button and it's working. If you have a phobia of anything computer related that's ok, but you'll have to shell out $2,000-$5,000 for a custom-made website if you're not willing to give it a try.

A FEW DEFINITIONS.
- Domain - The website address like www.dogtraining.com.

- HOSTING - The process of keeping your website files online for people to view. It's like online storage. Think iCloud for your website files and photos if you know what that is.

- SEO - SEARCH ENGINE OPTIMIZATION. SEO makes it easy for Google and other search engines to find you.

- TEMPLATE - A prefabricated program to stylize your website. A template gives you some basic formatting and colors to start with.

- AVERAGE SESSION TIME - The average time a new user spends on your website before leaving.

ANOTHER, less expensive, option would be to find a computer savvy friend and have them help you build your website. Even if they haven't made a website before, the two of you can figure it out with some of the tools I will list below.

. . .

Wix: A great option for someone who desires a really simple process. I would suggest the $10 a month option. It includes a domain name that you can choose, no ads and plenty of other options. You get the domain and hosting included.

Squarespace: Another simple option with elegant website templates to choose from. The $16 a month option will get you everything you'll need. You get the domain and hosting included.

Wordpress: My preferred platform for making websites. Wordpress powers 29% of all websites on the internet. It's free, but you'll need to get a domain and a hosting plan from a hosting company like bluehost.com. Wordpress shines above all the others when it comes to SEO. Google loves Wordpress websites. Wordpress will require a little more practice and research to make a nice website, but if you want some more advanced options on your website, this is a good choice. The cost is around $14 a month for hosting and domain from bluehost.com, and the Wordpress comes free with your hosting package.

99 designs is an awesome way to get things like websites, business cards, and logos. Their business model still blows my mind and I've used the company many times for new projects. Start by creating an account. If you want a website, post your project and thousands of designers from around the world will start making you a sample. Each designer is trying to impress you with their design so that you will choose them and your payment will be given to them to complete the project. I typically get about 80 designs to choose from when I post a project, which is so much better than paying one designer to create something for you that you may or may not like. www.99designs.com

What good is a beautiful website if nobody sees it? SEO is essential for your website. Very few people spend an ounce of time or money on this step, and it's a shame. You could spend $50,000 on an incredible website, and it would be a complete waste of money if people can't find your website via Google search.

IF YOU'RE on the Wordpress platform, there is a free plugin called Yoast SEO that does a decent job for some basic SEO. If your website is not doing well on Google, the best investment you can make is in SEO. I use a company called The Hoth. (www.thehoth.com) Their powerful link building service is a great starting place and under $300. Also see local citations. They also have other services depending on your business requirements. They have incredible customer service and will be able to help you if you don't know what to buy.

GOOGLE Adwords

Google Adwords is hands down the most effective tool to help dog trainers get new clients. It's an advertising platform that allows you to purchase clicks to your website when someone types in a keyword or phrase that they desire to learn more about. If I were a dog trainer in Memphis, Tennessee, I might choose a phrase like "dog trainer Memphis Tennessee." Google will then show an advertisement to any people searching that phrase. Essentially Google Adwords allows you to bypass natural search options by paying for priority.

YOU DON'T PAY if the potential client does not click on the ad. It's normal to pay about $2.50-$3 per click. You might be thinking that's incredibly expensive, right? Wrong. It's a qualified click. We know that the person who clicked on your ad has a dog, lives in your city, needs training and is seeking a service like yours! Prior to starting your ad campaign, you can set a budget to ensure that you don't exceed your desired advertising allotment, and you can stop your ads at any time.

. . .

Don't underestimate the fact that these are qualified leads. Every other type of advertising is driven by mass advertising with the hopes that the people who see the ad will be people who desire to see your ad. This is the main differentiating factor that sets Google Adwords apart. Google Adwords sells you clicks from people who are actually searching instead of spamming people with ads in hopes that they will click on your link.

I've yet to meet a dog trainer who was unhappy with their experience with Google Adwords. If you need help getting set up on Google Adwords, sign up for a free account and then give them a call and ask for help setting up your first campaign. They have excellent customer service that is willing to help you focus your advertising.

Facebook Advertising

Facebook ads offer the ability to place your ads in front of people with specific interests, in specified locations, gender and ages but they are not qualified clicks. Facebook ads are shown to people who did not ask to be shown your ad. They didn't seek your company; your company was seeking them. This is why a typical Facebook ad campaign could show your ads to thousands of potential clients in your area and you might not see a significant increase in calls or emails despite the ads. Nonetheless, Facebook ads are great for your brand awareness.

Facebook ads can reach a significant number of potential clients for a relatively small investment. A nice feature of Facebook ads is that they offer you the ability to optimize your ads for several different metrics. If you want more page likes on your business Facebook page, you can run ads that will help get you more followers. If you want to get people to call you on the phone, there is an option for that too. Business Facebook pages are great for doing live Q&A's with clients and potential clients. If you're new to Facebook and want to learn how to harness the power of Facebook for your business, I would highly recommend Courtney Foster Donahue's online training courses. Courtney is married to a dog trainer and she has several really exceptional online courses that can teach you how to master Facebook marketing. www.courtneyfosterdonahue.com

Your website

How much time do you think people will spend on your website? It's probably a lot less time than you think. In February 2016, my website's average session time was just one minute and fifty-five seconds. After a year of changes and upgrades, I was able to increase the average session time to two minutes and twenty-two seconds. You'll never have people's undivided attention for forty-five minutes, so don't bother trying. You should focus on what people need to see. People want to know if you can help them, how much you charge, they want to see social proof (testimonials) and how to contact you.

Forcing people to fill out long forms on your website is about as good for your business as the great depression. Build the relationship first, then ask them to do work. Your website should be simple and to the point. Having built more than sixty websites over the years, I can tell you that what dog trainers think they need on their website is almost never what they need. Purge. Spring clean. You don't need half of what your website has on it. Your website should have a home page, pricing or services and contact information. Anything else is probably just going to be excessive. More is almost never better with websites.

I have access to plenty of analytics for dog trainers' websites and it always shocks them to see the click trail, where potential clients go on their websites. It's always the same. Google leads them to the home page, then they click on the services/pricing page, then the contact page. About pages don't get any internet love. Blogs, training methodology and photo galleries just aren't what people click on. Make it easy for people to find your contact information, put it at the top of each page. Your home page should have about 75% of the information they need to know on it and this is not an excuse to have a cluttered home page.

A GREAT WEBSITE that sells is simple. It has a home page, a services/pricing page, testimonials page, and a contact page.

YOUR SERVICES PAGE doesn't need to have prices on it, but it does need to have your phone number with instructions to call or email you to set up a free evaluation. Most people can understand that each dog is an individual and that could require different pricing depending on the dog at hand. I don't have stock prices; it depends on the dog I'm training and how long I think the process will take. The two goals of your website is to give people hope and to get them to call you.

Do yourself a favor and call the local community college and see if they have a photography class. If they do, ask them if they can set you up with a few students to take photos for your business. Often you can get this done for free because aspiring photographers need photos in their portfolios. If you can't get free photos, then call a local professional photographer and get some nice photos done with your dog or dogs. I can't express how beneficial professional photos have been for my business. It's an easy way to set yourself apart from your competition and show the world that you're a professional and that you take your business and brand seriously.

ON YOUR SERVICES/PRICING page, you'll want to offer some information about your programs. Offer no more than four program options and list the prices only for the lower priced options. When writing out the information about your programs, it's critical to include the features and benefits of each program. Features are what the client gets and the benefits are how the features make them feel. For more on this concept of features and benefits, you can read *Book Yourself Solid* by Michael Port.

Let's look at an example.

ABC DOG TRAINERS off-leash freedom program:

• Five private lessons with your trainer in the comfort of your home

• ONE YEAR of weekly drop-in classes for maintenance

• ANY TRAINING TOOLS are included in the price of our programs

• PERSONALIZED weekly homework and check-ins

DO you want to be able to trust your dog off leash? You know your dog needs a good run off leash every day, but the backyard just isn't giving him or her what they need anymore. Don't worry because our off-leash freedom program has been able to help dogs of every breed to have off-leash freedom. We make it easy by coming to your home for training. When your dog is excelling with the training, you can both transition into our weekly drop-in classes free of charge for one year to ensure that the training works in new environments with plenty of distractions. Won't it be nice to let your dog have the freedom they used to have? We personalize each program for each dog and client. Off-leash freedom is a phone call away. Call us today, and we'll book a time to meet for a free evaluation in the comfort of your home to talk about training options and pricing. Chat soon! Mary Campbell (111)-222-3333

. . .

MORE WAYS TO *increase your income*

Having a strong referral system in place to consistently deliver you great clients is one method of making more income in your business, but it's not the entire story. You can also increase the lifetime value of those clients. A practical application of this is to upsell your clients on other services or products that you might sell in addition to your main training programs. Selling dog food is a great way to maximize your lifetime value of your clients. The great thing about selling dog food is that it's a consumable product which means that your clients don't buy it once, they buy it once every few weeks.

IF YOU HAD fifty clients sign up in year one and their average lifetime value was $1,000 for training, you could add something like food sales and increase that lifetime value to $1,500 or more just by adding food sales to your business.

ANOTHER WAY TO increase the lifetime value of a client is to start a joint venture with other dog-related businesses in your area. If you have a local friend who's a veterinarian or owns a boarding facility, you could arrange a one time or recurring affiliate revenue by taking 10% of the sales those business make from clients you refer. I've even done this with another local trainer. When you get too busy and can't take new clients, you can refer them to another trainer and charge that trainer $20 for each referral.

IN REALITY, I would probably send those clients to that trainer regardless because it's in my nature to offer substitutions to other services because I want all dog owners to have access to the best services possible. It's easy to set up by having the other business print out a basic business card with a promotion such as "Get $20 off your first vet visit" and give it to your clients. When the clients book the first visit, they get a discount, and the Vet knows to credit your business with the referral. Often these ventures are run on the trust that the joint venture company will do the right thing and pay you the money they agreed to for each referral. This new income stream is a simple way to leverage the trust you have already built with existing clients.

PROFESSIONAL ASSOCIATION MEMBERSHIPS:

There are many professional dog training associations that you can support and at the same time use to show your potential clients that you are focused on ongoing education. When you join these organizations, they typically give you a certificate that you can hang up in your office or allow you to place their logo on your website to show your affiliation. Some of these organizations don't have requirements to prove that you are an expert and some do. Several also have training courses that you can do to achieve training achievement and designations for further prominence. Here are a few organizations that might be of interest to you.

- http://www.canineprofessionals.com/

- https://apdt.com/

- http://www.cappdt.ca/

- http://www.ipdta.org/

IF YOU ARE LIKING this book, you can find Thriving Dog Trainers Book 2 also on Amazon; Thriving Dog Trainers Book 2: Get better clients, work less, enjoy your life and business

ACCESS your free business resources here: http://www.tedsbooks.com/trainer-docs

BLOW THEIR MINDS

Your job as a dog trainer is to motivate the humans in a way that resonates with them. If you get nothing else from this book, please focus on this. If you got into dog training because you can't stand people and love working with dogs, you'll always struggle in the dog training industry. The plain and simple truth is that working with people is not optional. You can limit your human interaction by focusing on board and train clients, but you'll still need to train the owners and do follow-up training along the way after the dog goes home. Like it or not, the humans have the credit cards, and those credit cards put food on your table.

THE MOST FINANCIALLY SUCCESSFUL dog trainers I know are not the best dog trainers I know. They have learned the art of dancing with the client. How to sell dog training, how to connect with people, how to listen to people's needs, and how to over-deliver on their promises. These are all skills you'll want to develop if you don't already have them. You can outsource marketing to a marketing company, but you can't outsource your personality and your ability to win people over.

. . .

THESE SKILLS ARE JUST as essential to learn as your dog training abilities. I've had the great privilege of helping educate thousands of dog trainers from around the world and over and over, I see the same mindset. These well-meaning business owners say they want to learn sales, marketing, and personal development and yet when given a choice between two education products, they overwhelmingly choose the dog training education product over a business course.

WHY IS THIS? It's because they know they need to learn about business, but they didn't get into dog training so that they could be a business owner, they went into dog training because they wanted to train dogs all day. Unfortunately for them, this isn't how dog training works. Unless you work for a training company as an employee, the chances are you'll spend at least half of your day answering emails, booking clients, acquiring new clients, making videos to promote your business, filing your paperwork, updating your website and other random tasks like these. Knowing what you're signing up for is an important part of having realistic expectations about what your day to day will look like. You're a business owner who just happens to train dogs. Welcome to the tribe. For more on business, life, sales, and personal development come check out our facebook group called Thriving Dog Trainers. You can find a link here: www.tedsbooks.com/trainer-docs

THE MAJORITY of my clients have trained with one to five other trainers before landing on me. There are plenty of reasons things might not have worked out with previous trainers, but when they call me, they get the red carpet. I answer the phone with a pleasant "Hello, Ted the dog trainer, how can I help you?" I'm sure to write down their first name and dogs on a scrap piece of paper the moment they introduce themselves so that I can address them by name during our conversation. This is a great tip for people like me who are terrible with names. My entire goal when I talk to someone who is calling me is to offer them hope.

. . .

Most potential clients who call me are feeling hopeless and I choose to be the football coach who gives them hope that all is not lost. You can do the same in your business. You know something interesting I've found across all of my clients? Almost every one of them think their dog is terrible and untrainable. I'm always sure to remind myself to tell them that I can help. Clearly, if you are at the place in your career where you lack confidence and experience you wouldn't want to give people false hope. Just be honest with them, tell them you want to help and offer to train for free or for a small fee with a full refund if you can't help.

I listen to them and let them vent if they want to. I don't try to sell them anything, I listen, ask questions and take notes. Being genuinely interested in their story and situation is important here. When they feel that they have told me everything, it's my turn to talk. I typically start by telling them that I've worked with many dogs just like theirs and then suggest that we meet so that I can meet their dog before giving them a proper quote and program structure. Offering an in-person meeting is not necessarily required for potential clients looking for basic services like group classes or puppy training, but I do highly suggest either a comprehensive free phone consultation or an in-person free evaluation. As mentioned several times in this book already, under-promise and over-deliver from the first email to the last hug.

The way you make people feel is astonishingly critical. People are frustrated with their dogs and are opening up to you, so you should have the self-awareness to see that they are actually taking a big leap just by picking up the phone. Be patient and treat them like they are a close friend who is struggling in their marriage. Have empathy for people. People tend to leave these calls to the last minute because our society tells us to be independent. It's our job to let them know that everything is going to be ok; they need that reassurance. Roll out the red carpet.

MANGO DOGS IS GROWING and we'll help you get up to speed on your dog training skills, handle all of your marketing and you'll be part of our team. For more information go to: www.mangodogs.com/join

GET THE REFERRAL

Word-of-mouth referrals have the most power to influence a potential client. If that referral comes from a trusted friend or professional, it will hold even more weight as the potential client is deciding if they need help. But not all referrals are created equally.

VETERINARIANS

The Formula teaches its followers to seek the veterinarian referral above all else. The reasons are simple.

- VETERINARIANS HAVE daily access to dozens of new potential clients.

- VETS HAVE to deal with the bad behaviors of their canine clients and so it's in their best interest to promote a trusted trainer.

- A REFERRAL from a veterinarian holds an incredible amount of weight because dog owners trust their veterinarian.

. . .

BUILDING a referral network from veterinarians can be incredibly intimidating for people and I know that it was for me initially, but trust me when I say that the incredible benefits will greatly outweigh the costs. You can find a free pdf and audiobook on my website that will guide you through the process of getting vets to refer clients to your business. www.tedsbooks.com/trainer-docs

A FEW YEARS AGO, I started noticing a trend that I would never have seen coming. In the years prior, I had received a significant amount of referrals directly from clients that I didn't expect would give me a good referral. These referrals were coming from the 5% of my clients that I didn't feel did a great job. These were the 5% that didn't even finish the training. They did about three-quarters of the training and just fizzled out. I never heard from them again, they didn't come to any of the free drop-in group classes and they just disappeared. Still, to this day I don't know why I get so many referrals from them, but I have asked other successful trainers, and many of them have also seen this phenomenon as well. Never discount the ability of mediocre clients to give you a glowing review despite how well you think they did with the training.

EVERY PHONE CALL and evaluation that you do, you should ask people how they heard about your business. This is a critical step that will help you see where your marketing is being effective and where it's not producing any tangible results.

WHEN A PREVIOUS CLIENT refers your business, you should really consider further incentivizing, so that they continue to refer. A hand-written letter in the mail is a free option, or an Amazon gift card can also be a nice way to say thanks. I send out thank you cards with beautiful photos of my dogs on the cards. The cards thank them for supporting my business with referrals. Sometimes just a simple card and a thank you is all it takes to keep the referrals coming.

Testimonials

Testimonials are the lifeblood of a dog training business. While many of my fellow dog trainers blow their clients' minds, they often struggle to get testimonials from them. There are a few reasons why well meaning-clients struggle to produce a testimonial even after being repeatedly reminded. The two biggest reasons why people put it off is because they either don't know what to write or are really busy. Here's the fix. Towards the end of training, when the client is extremely happy and beaming with pride, ask them for a testimonial. I've never had someone say no. What I do next is the key. I ask them to do one now. I take out a camera and snap a few photos and tell them they can do the testimonial by recording it onto my voice recorder. Most smartphones have a camera and voice recorder built into them.

I OUTLINE for them what a testimonial is. A testimonial is just answering three questions.

1. What was your dog like before training?

2. WHAT IS your dog like now?

3. WOULD you refer our company to your friends and family?

I HIT record and tell them I will be back in five minutes so that they don't feel self-conscious. This method handles the two issues we discussed above: not having time and not knowing what to write. This little tip has produced countless testimonials for my business, so give it a try.

. . .

IT'S RECOMMENDED to get as much breed variety as you can in your testimonials. Over the years, I've had many potential clients call me asking for help because they saw a testimonial on my website that resonated with them. They often will say they read a specific testimonial and that's why they called. Don't underestimate how much breed will affect a potential clients desire to pick up the phone. If you only have testimonials with German Shepherds, you'll mainly get calls about German Shepherds and the same can be said for any breed. Mixing up your breed variety in testimonials is important.

ACCESS your free business resources here: http://www.tedsbooks.com/trainer-docs

GET TO WORK

TO DO LIST

*E*verything you just read will prove to be useless in your business if you don't do anything with it. The action is the differentiating factor that will decide if your business crawls or runs. Take as much from this book as you like, but don't underestimate the power of having a proven system to follow. I've seen this system help thousands of dogs trainers build amazing businesses and it can do the same for you if you're willing to put in the time and do the work. Don't be afraid to change.

[ ] Get the proper permits for your business, registration, and insurance.

[ ] Do the market research to find out who you need to be marketing to.

[ ] Make sure you are up to date on your training techniques.

. . .

[ ] Pick a main business model and the services you will provide.

[ ] Decide how much you will charge for your services.

[ ] Consider evaluations to hone your sales skills and increase business revenue.

[ ] Which social media will you commit to? Stick to one or two.

[ ] Build your website or simplify the one you already have.

[ ] Setup a Google Adwords account to drive qualified traffic to your website.

[ ] Take steps to increase website traffic with SEO.

[ ] Examine your business to see if you can increase your clients lifetime value, resulting in more revenue.

[ ] Have you joined any professional training associations yet?

[ ] Examine your business and see how you can set it apart from your competition.

[ ] Get as many testimonials as you possibly can. Train dogs for free if you need to!

[ ] Spend time each week building your veterinarian referral system.

Haters

Unfortunately, the dog training industry is full of extremists.

For many years, I was ruthlessly attacked by other dog trainers. If you find yourself being attacked like I was, here are a few tips on how to navigate these waters.

1. As hard as it is, I always ask myself if there is any truth to what these people are saying. If the answer is yes, you will need to up your game.
2. Limit the amount they can pick on you. You can tweak the settings on your YouTube account to automatically disable comments every time you post a new video. Disable the five-star rating system on your business Facebook page, as people who have never worked with you can post nasty fake reviews.
3. Avoid Yelp at all costs. No need to say more. Just look up the company and some of the unethical business decisions they have made and are still committed to.
4. Do not engage with these haters. That's what they want; they want to get under your skin. It's just like Junior High all over again. The insecure kids make fun of the more secure kids to make themselves feel better about their low self-worth. Being combative with them will only add fuel to the fire.
5. Remember that haters don't actually take business away from people. All the hate I had thrown at me back in the day only brought me website traffic and that traffic turned into dogs that needed to be trained. My wife reminded me of this. Every year, my business doubled or tripled despite the haters.

6. Avoid acting defensively via legal action unless you absolutely have to. Defamation of character is something that will look really tempting to file, but avoiding these people tends to work better. Worst case scenario, have your lawyer send them a cease and desist letter, that should be more than enough.
7. When to go to the authorities? If they threaten your life, call the police immediately.
8. Try and meet with them for coffee. Most of them will not be willing to do so... but the ones that are may lay off you if they meet you in person. Once you meet someone, it becomes personal. I know this has helped me a lot over the years!
9. Pray for them.

Boundaries

Boundaries are hard to define but essential for having a thriving business over the long term. When I take on a new client, they are told when they can contact me for help. I love working and train clients from Monday through Saturday. My clients know not to contact me on Sundays unless they are willing to leave a message or wait for an email response on Monday. They're informed of my utter disdain for text messaging and that I don't get texts on my phone. Now I know what you're thinking... Don't text with my clients? You've lost it, Ted! Hear me out. Texting has very different expectations associated with it. People expect that you'll return a text within an hour. If you open that text and don't respond promptly, some smartphones allow the recipient to see that you opened that text and have yet to respond. I'll pass on that method of communication.

Surprisingly, I've been ridiculed for this in the past, and I'm fine with that; it's just a suggestion. Maybe a story will help illustrate my position on texting with clients. A friend of mine, a very talented dog trainer, posted recently on a secret dog training facebook page that she had accidentally texted one of her clients a very sexual text message by accident. She thought that message was bound for her husband, but it ended up on the phone of one of her male clients. Ouch. If you don't draw the line early, you might find yourself in an endless cascade of texts. Just be careful to set boundaries if you decide to text with clients. Having a personal cell phone and a business cell phone is an easy way to avoid overlap between business and home life.

NEVER EMOTIONALLY INVEST MORE into the success of a client's dog than the client is willing to invest. I can't stress this point enough. You see the dog's potential, you know he wants to learn and change, but his owners are on the fence. They find it hard to commit to the success of their dog and you're fighting for this dog. Let me commend you for your devotion to helping these dogs but it's only going to lead to unmet expectations on your part. As it's said, "You can lead a horse to water but you can't make him drink." If you don't take this advice, you might find yourself up late at night questioning why you're even trying to help dogs. It takes two to tango, and it takes two to train a dog successfully.

WHERE DO THE HOURS GO?

One of the things that most dog trainers struggle with is the transition from part-time to full-time. No more boss and nobody keeping them accountable. Be industrious with your time. Most jobs have objectives and goals that have to be met each day/week/month. When that structure is left behind, it can be a real challenge to keep on track. Time mapping is a great way to determine where the hours go in the day. On a typical day, grab a notebook and log what you are doing every 30 minutes from the moment you get out of bed to the moment you go back to sleep. You may be surprised by how much time you waste on things that don't actually make a difference in your business.

Here are a few ideas on how to keep from getting lazy and feeling defeated.

- Each day, each week, and each month, you'll need a to-do list.
- Each day should incorporate a combination of dog training, emails, phone calls and marketing your business.
- DO NOT check your email more than three times a day, you can do your emails in batches.
- DO NOT go on Facebook or other social media platforms more than two times a day. This pattern gone unchecked can make people extremely unproductive. Social media and email are great ways to hide from real work.
- You must do at least one thing each day to market your business. This step can't be overlooked, never stop marketing even if you're busy.
- If you find yourself avoiding work, you'll need a friend to call you weekly to keep you accountable.

THINK of business like an escalator that's going down and you're walking up the escalator trying to get to the top. What happens if you stop walking up the escalator? You go down with the escalator. Your legs need to have more stamina than the motor that's taking you down. The escalator is your competition. Don't stop advertising, don't stop getting testimonials, don't stop blowing people's minds. If you do, you're likely to be overcome by your competition. Never stop innovating, never stop tweaking your services, never stop caring about your clients.

REVIEW the to-do list and the anatomy of *The Formula* to define what your next steps should be.

1. Learn dog training skills
2. Pick the right business model
3. Find clients
4. Blow their minds
5. Get referrals

ARE YOU CONTINUING YOUR EDUCATION? Have you picked a great business model that's working for you? Are you focusing on marketing your business consistently? Are you truly offering a business that's remarkable? Are you utilizing your past clients and veterinarians to get more referrals? *The Formula* works, but if you're missing one or more of the steps, it will feel like you're not getting any traction. Do the hard work, it will pay off.

ALLOW me to offer a warm thank you for reading this book. My desire is for nothing but prosperity and happiness and would love to hear from you if you need help along the way!

Check out our website, sign up for my email newsletter so that you will be informed when I release new books and join our Facebook page. I often have mastermind training courses for dog trainers and you can find the supplemental documents for this book there as well. It's with great honor that I get to help dog trainers with their businesses and would love to hear from you.

THE KNOWLEDGE that I've shared with you is in large part ideas that I have learned by doing things incorrectly. Never be afraid to look back on your past mistakes and learn from them, just as I have. For an evaluation form you can use in your business, go to: http://www.tedsbooks.com/trainer-docs

THANK YOU!

If you have questions, feel free to email me personally, I love helping out dog owners and trainers. Email: ted@tedsbooks.com.

Don't forget to review the book on Amazon, it really helps me out!!! Thanks in advance.

Ted Efthymiadis

- *Access all of your free resources + audiobook*
- *Join the mailing list*
- *Find all of my other books*
- *Access online training sessions with me*
- *At www.tedsbooks.com*

MANGO DOGS IS GROWING and we'll help you get up to speed on your dog training skills, handle all of your marketing and you'll be part of our team. For more information go to: www.mangodogs.com/join

ALSO BY TED EFTHYMIADIS

All titles are available on Amazon in Kindle and Physical book some, some are available in audiobook version from www.audible.com

Thriving Dog Trainers Book 2: Get better clients, work less, enjoy your life and business

Giving Up On My Dog: A straightforward directive for those close to giving up on their dog

Potty Training Puppy: A comprehensive guide to help you navigate the crappy job of house training your puppy

E-COLLAR TRAINING for Pet Dogs: The only resource you'll need to train your dog with the aid of an electric training collar

Manufactured by Amazon.ca
Bolton, ON